WE BRITS

John Agard was born in Guyana and came to Britain in 1977. He has published two collections with Serpent's Tail, *Mangoes and Bullets* and *Lovelines for a Goat-Born Lady*, and three with Bloodaxe, *From the Devil's Pulpit* (1997), *Weblines* (2000) and *We Brits* (2006). He is a popular children's writer whose titles include *Get Back Pimple* (Viking), *Laughter is an Egg* (Puffin), *Grandfather's Old Bruk-a-down Car* (Red Fox), *I Din Do Nuttin* (Red Fox), *Points of View with Professor Peekaboo* (Bodley Head) and *We Animals Would Like a Word with You* (Bodley Head), which won a Smarties Award. *Einstein, The Girl Who Hated Maths*, a collection inspired by mathematics, and *Hello H2O*, a collection inspired by science, were published by Hodder Children's Books and illustrated by Satoshi Kitamura.

His most recent collection, *Half-Caste* (Hodder Children's Books, 2004), includes the poem 'Half-Caste', studied by countless GCSE students and which he has performed with GCSE Poetry Live to thousands across the country.

He won the Casa de las Américas Prize in 1982 for *Man to Pan*, and in 1997 was one of the five poets given the Paul Hamlyn Award for Poetry. He was also twice winner of the Guyana Prize, for *From the Devil's Pulpit* and *Weblines*.

As a touring speaker with the Commonwealth Institute, he visited nearly 2000 schools promoting Caribbean culture and poetry, and has performed on television and around the world. In 1989 he was awarded an Arts Council Bursary and in 1993 became the first Writer in Residence at London's South Bank Centre, who published *A Stone's Throw from Embankment*, a collection written during that residency. In 1998 he was writer-in-residence for the BBC with the Windrush project, and Bard at the Beeb, a selection of poems written during that residency, was published by BBC Learning Support.

He has recently collaborated with Bob Cattell on *Butter-Finger* (Frances Lincoln, 2005), a cricket novel for children to which he contributed calypso cricket poems.

He has also written plays. He lives with the poet Grace Nichols and family in Sussex, and they received the CLPE Poetry Award 2003 for *Under the Moon and Over the Sea* (Walker Books), a children's anthology they co-edited.

JOHN AGARD

We Brits

BLOODAXE BOOKS

ISBN: 1 85224 733 9

First published 2006 by
Bloodaxe Books Ltd,
Highgreen,
Tarset,
Northumberland NE48 1RP.

www.bloodaxebooks.com
For further information about Bloodaxe titles
please visit our website or write to
the above address for a catalogue.

Bloodaxe Books Ltd acknowledges
the financial assistance of
Arts Council England, North East.

ARTS COUNCIL ENGLAND

Cover printing by J. Thomson Colour Printers Ltd, Glasgow.

Printed in Great Britain by
Bell & Bain Limited, Glasgow.

For Grace

And the memory of St Raphael's Way Neasden
where we stayed with Dad and Mama Coreen on arrival
And to Reinhard Sander and Christopher Wrigley
who opened a door to the Sussex Downs

And to Deo Persaud for those Notting Hill carnival days
And to John LaRose's university kitchen
And the Bogle-L'Ouverture back-a-yard
gatherings of Eric and Jessica Huntley

And Marc and Kamal's Knatchbull Road church house dos
where Aubrey's pan and Keith's flute sweetened the lime
And not forgetting Barbara's spamming Offham get-togethers
And Beck's Robin Hood style barbeques on the Rise

And Bari dreaming of the big one round the corner
And Mark plotting live literature in dark October

And last but not least the rest of the Lewes posse

And to friendships in all weathers

ACKNOWLEDGEMENTS

'Toussaint L'Ouverture Acknowledges Wordsworth's Sonnet "To Toussaint L'Ouverture"' first appeared in *'Earth has not any thing to shew more fair': a bicentenary celebration of Wordsworth's sonnet 'Composed upon Westminster Bridge, 3 Sept. 1802*, edited by Peter Oswald, Alice Oswald and Robert Woof (Shakespeare's Globe and The Wordsworth Trust, 2002).

'Dialogue' was commissioned by the English-speaking Union and read at Westminster Abbey for the ESU's 85th anniversary on 26 June 2003, thanks to Valerie Mitchell.

'Roll Over Your Bones Creech Jones' was first published in *The Independent* in 1998, marking the 50th anniversary of the arrival in Britain of the *Empire Windrush* and to launch the BBC Windrush writer's residency, thanks to an idea of Jeffery Morris.

'Memo to Professor Enoch Powell' first appeared in *The Independent* in 1998.

'Love Calls Us Back from Simplification' first appeared in *A Stone's Throw from Embankment* (Royal Festival Hall, 1993), thanks to Christina Patterson.

'Testing Time' first appeared in *Poetry Review* in 1999, edited by Peter Forbes).

'On a Yazoo Stem' first appeared in *The POT Anthology* (New Departures, 2005), edited by Michael Horovitz.

I'm indebted to the authors of a number of eye-opening books including *The Letters of Ignatius Sancho*, ed. Paul Edwards & Polly Rewt, foreword by David Dabydeen (Edinburgh University Press, 1994); *The Wonderful Adventures of Mrs Seacole in Many Lands*, ed. Ziggy Alexander (Falling Wall Press, 1984); *Batting for the Empire: A Political Biography of Ranjitsinhji*, by Mario Rodrigues (Penguin Books India, 2003); *Staying Power: The History of Black People in Britain* by Peter Fryer (Pluto Press, 1984); *Culture & Imperialism* by Edward W. Said (Chatto & Windus, 1993); *The Ingenius Mr Fairchild: The Father of the Flower Garden* by Michael Lepman (Headline, 2000).

Thanks to Paul Taylor for the photo.

CONTENTS

Queue

O please don't knock the good old British queue.
It gives a fair turn to anonymous me and you.

Weather

No other nation does it better.
Weather-talk is our raison d'être.

True Grit

Here comes a black Englishman with a brolly.
To forget either would indeed be folly.

Gandhi's Revenge

Those Brit tastebuds are in for a morale boost.
Chicken tikka massala is home to roost.

Metric Sceptic

He'd rather lay Shakespeare's bones in Notre Dame
than weigh his Cox's apples in kilograms.

Ethnic Eccentric

Lighten up, afto-centrics, it's too easy to deride
A monocled black Brit in jodhpurs going for a ride.

Moorish

The more the Morris Dancers strut their knees
And flash their swords, the more the Moors are pleased.

Rewards Ahoy!

What's in store for pirates licensed to loot?
A knighthood and a twenty-two gun salute.

The Blond Sheep in the Family

John Bull Junior, not quite a chip off the old block.
Did one educate him to be a blond dreadlock?

Mixed Marriages

Mixed marriages do have their advantages.
We express our needs and tiffs in two languages.

What More Can One Ask of Cricket?

To bridge continents with glorious uncertainty.
To leave a legacy of unpredictability.

A Whiff of Nationhood

Churchill once said fish and chips make good companions.
We Welsh say the same of folk from the Mabinogion.

Just for the Record

We Scots gave them the light bulb, the telephone, the telly.
Now, how about a haggis rocket launched to the belly.

A Dark Brew

No problem too big for a pint of Guinness.
A drop can drown political correctness.

Subliminally Yours

Our subconscious feeds on a subcontinent's spices
Even while munching Mr Kipling's almond slices.

Post-Independence Reminders

We gave them the English language, we gave them parades.
Our lingo will linger long after the bugle fades.

Dialogue

Out of a scattering of tongues
out of Babel's inheritance

How reassemble sense
from this gift of rich confusion?

How resurrect a rainbow
from a tower of ruins?

How begin to begin
the dance of utterance?

So armed with my hybrid dictionary
– a not so concise Oxford –

I face the wilderness of the Word,
letting English be my bridge

to a world harvest –
a gathering from continents

retracing empire's footsteps
seeking this time not global glory

but dialogue in the distance.

Roll Over Your Bones Creech Jones

They must be allowed to land They have British passports. There's nothing to worry about. They won't last one winter in England.'

CREECH JONES, then colonial secretary,
on the wave of Caribbean emigration
after the arrival of the *Windrush* in 1948

Roll over your bones Creech Jones

I've learnt to read between the lines of ice
for footnotes of spring

and dare to face the draught
armed with my old ancestral scarf

Roll over your bones Creech Jones

I've lit a black candle in the house
of an English winter

sprinkled white rum on altars of snow

and passed the microphone to my shadow

Roll over your bones Creech Jones

From Britannia To Whom It May Concern

Thank you for the kind thought, the compliment
of even calling me mother country.
You make an island feel like a continent.

When I ruled the waves, all the world seemed pink.
I manipulated maps with sword and cross.
Shifted boundaries with seal of royal ink.

I enthroned my language as a rule of tongue.
Gathered India's jewels into my crown.
And Africa's blood still haunts my monuments.

How can I turn from history's looking-glass
when even my sugar holds a bitter past?
The sea has been my girdle and my guilt.

Though darkness enriches my red white and blue,
I've learnt how the sun sets on empires.
And the voiceless voice their righteous fires.

Now, old ruptures bless me with hybrid webs.
I feel horizons throbbing at my doorstep.
My streets pulse with a plurality of tongues.

And mother country has much work to do.
I must prepare my cliffs for new homecomings.
Tie yellow ribbons round my children's minds.

The Ascent of John Edmonstone

(The freed black slave who taught Darwin taxidermy at Edinburgh – 1826.)

My name rings no bell
in the ears of science
but footnotes know me well –

footnotes where history
shows its true colours
and passing reference is flesh

for I am John Edmonstone,
whose name is little known
to evolution's white ladder.

But Darwin will remember me,
just say the black man who taught him
Egypt's ancient art of taxidermy.

To think that we should meet
in Edinburgh of all places
few doors apart on Lothian Street.

No mention then of savage races.
In those days we were two bird-stuffers
mounting mortality in feathers.

We were each other's missing link
colleagues upright on the chain of being
a pair of wingless apes condemned to think.

Ignacio Sancho Returns the Compliment

A white fellow once said in praise of me:
'God's image, though cut in ebony.'
And I, a dark fellow, said of him kindly:
'God's image, though cut in ivory.'

Oh! The pleasures of novelty to youth! – we went by water –
had a coach home – were gazed at – followed &c. &c. –
but not much abused.
– The Letters of Ignatius Sancho, 27 August 1777

Newton's Amazing Grace

*(John Newton [1725-1807], slave ship captain, who converted to
the ministry and composed many hymns, including 'Amazing Grace'.)*

Grace is not a word for which I had much use.
And I skippered ships that did more than bruise
the face of the Atlantic. I carved my name
in human cargo without a thought of shame.
But the sea's big enough for a man to lose
his conscience, if not his puny neck.
In the sea's eye, who is this upstart speck
that calls himself a maker of history?
It took a storm to save the dumb wretch in me.
On a night the winds weighed heavy as my sins,
I spared a thought for those poor souls below deck.
Terror made rough waters my Damascus road.
Amazing grace began to lead me home.
Lord, let my soul's scum be measured by a hymn.

Ave Eliza

Her Majestie understanding that there are of late
divers blackmoores brought into this realme,
of which kinde people there are already to manie...
QUEEN ELIZABETH I, 11 JULY 1596

On horseback facing her troops at Tilbury,
she proclaimed a feeble woman's body
blessed with the heart and stomach of a king.
Queen of a kingdom. No common weakling
with pre-menstrual cramps and a weak bladder.
Let all who doubt remember the Armada.
That upstart from Spain, he got off lightly.
A singed beard on a monarch looks unsightly.
And that French dude who pestered for a snog,
she packed him to Anjou and called him her 'Frog'.
Though too much sugar had pillaged her teeth,
Hilliard's brush would keep her portrait sweet.
Till death her legs she would not part. Kept pure
for a realm growing motley with Blackamoors.

Memo to Professor Enoch Powell

In the name of Alpha and Omega
I address you, Professor Enoch Powell.
Shall I forward this to heaven or to hell?
What's immigration like in the afterlife?

Did St Peter hassle you at the pearly gates?
Or Satan question your right to immigrate?
Say you have nothing to declare but your dust
and your ghost may yet gain refugee status.

It must be a supernatural culture shock,
even for a classical scholar,
to meet angels in turbans and haloes of dreadlocks
carousing along eternity's corridors.

And clovenfoot men in bowler hats
waving their tridents like union jacks.
But since you yourself were not averse to verse,
where paradox blesses and purity is a curse,

I'll quote, Professor, from your own words:
'The flocks of migrant birds,
They are all poems...' But alas
your view of migration could only embrace

those feathered immigrants of space –
an example of what happens, Professor,
when the intellect's shining mirror
is cracked by a terror of the Other.

But as translator of the New Testament,
Paradise may yet grant you some reprieve.
Then again with the classics up your sleeve,
Dante's *Inferno* may prove your element.

Here, on earth, it's nearly spring.
February shimmers with rivers of blood
that still flow in the veins of black and white.
And migrant poems bloom in inner-city light.

'Every Prime Minister Needs a Willie'

*(Prime Minister Margaret Thatcher praising
her deputy Willie Whitelaw)*

When debating with all those men in grey,
a Willie on your side can go a long way.

Oh, a Willie is no doubt an asset
when a lady tops the Cabinet.

A Willie that can be relied on
will prove a thorn to the Opposition.

Tell the right honourable gentlemen
who gang up on her at Number 10

that when a lady prime minister
has a loyal Willie for a mentor

then the world of politics' her oyster.
Willie Whitelaw, say Aye if in favour.

Talking to Plants

Always talk to your plants.
Sit back and watch them flourish.
Good advice. Of course we presume
that all plants speak English.

Speak slowly, watch them bloom.
If necessary shout each syllable.
Their little ears are ready vessels
for a shower of the Queen's vowels.

Never mind if it's a China rose
or an African violet.
Better yet, recite a bit of English Lit.
See abundance spring at your fingertip.

So I spoke like an Oxford don
to my wilting rhododendron.
It wilted more. As for my drooping shrub,
my words only seem to draw more slugs.

O plants, what is it that makes you grow?
I watch my immigrant neighbour's patio
with a sense of distant envy.
Tell me, plants, must I address you in Punjabi?

Gentleman Gandhi

The guerrilla fighter whose gun was truth
the cotton-wielding consciousness-rouser
the dhoti-clad doorway to midnight's freedom
the little brown man Churchill loved to despise
the salty thorn in the British rosy side.

Because he knew that empire's map-pink glow
was but passing ash in Agni's fire.
And not a never-ending sunrise.
He who in London took up the violin.
He who in Delhi blessed his assassin.

See him now in a grey English drizzle
spinning the prayer wheel of an umbrella.
See him now treading a carpet of snow –
the subversive road of salt not yet taken.

Taking the Dogma for a Walk

Whatever its colour or its breed –
it's wise to keep your dogma on a lead
for many a dogma has been known
to settle for a human bone.

A dogma can turn on its owner.
A bit like what's called friendly fire.
A dogma can bite the hand that feeds it,
however much you shout *Sit! Sit!*

Dogmas tend to sniff other dogmas.
Then dogma joins dogma in heat.
This can happen on your own sofa
or in front of an entire street.

People, they say, begin to resemble
the dogma they keep for companion.
I watch my dogma's physiognomy
for traces of my own expression.

But it's not as easy as it sounds.
A dogma is good at disguising its mug.
Now a do-gooder, now a thug.
Both wagging with toothsome conviction.

Reporting from the Frontline of
the Great Dictionary Disaster

Why has the English dictionary grown so thin?
Why is it weeping between its covers?
Because today is the day
all words of foreign origin
return to their native borders.
Linguists are rioting in the streets.
Crossword lovers are on hunger strike.
But words are voting with their feet
and familiar objects across the British Isles
have staged a mass evacuation.

Anoraks
have been seen flying off backs
remaking their Innuit tracks.

Bananas
hands forming a queue
are now bound for a Bantu rendezvous.

Hammocks
leave bodies in mid-swing
and billow back to a Carib beginning.

Pyjamas
without regard to size or age
take off on a Hindu pilgrimage.

Sofas
huddle themselves into caravans,
their destination – the Arabian sands.

Even Baguettes
(as we speak) grab the chance
to jump the channel for the south of France.

This is a tragedy
turning into a comedy
for reports are reaching us by satellite
that in the wee hours of the night
the ghosts of ancient Greeks and Romans
have been preparing an epic knees-up
to mark the homecoming of their word-hoard.
Stay tuned for live and direct coverage
on this day a dictionary mourns its language.

Forever Afters

Served, as always, for the last.
The tail end of the menu.
The main course's epitaph.
A pudding knows the meaning
of waiting one's turn in queue.
Patience is what puddings know best.
And when all face the final test
on that day of reckoning,
puddings will array their glory
down to the smallest gooseberry,
for every pudding knows one truth –
that the first shall be last
and the last shall be first.
Yes, puddings shall have the last laugh
when the sweet inherits the tooth.

Alternative Anthem

Put the kettle on
Put the kettle on
It is the British answer
to Armageddon.

Never mind taxes rise
Never mind trains are late
One thing you can be sure of
and that's the kettle, mate.

It's not whether you lose
It's not whether you win
It's whether or not
you've plugged the kettle in.

May the kettle ever hiss
May the kettle ever steam
It is the engine
that drives our nation's dream.

Long live the kettle
that rules over us
May it be limescale free
and may it never rust.

Sing it on the beaches
Sing it from the housetops
The sun may set on empire
but the kettle never stops.

Tea with Earl Grey

I am the second Earl Grey, the first one begot.
When the conscience of Empire begins to rot,
I turn to Assam with a sniff of bergamot.

My rule saw the middle-class enfranchised, my friend.
Throughout our colonies, I sealed slavery's end.
But what shall I be remembered by? A tea blend.

Therapeutic Exercise with the Union Jack

Think red.
Think tongue.
Think one blood.

Think white.
Think bone.
Think one skeleton.

Think blue.
Think sea.
Think one sky.

Now try
thinking back.

Think black.
Think night.
Think word.

Think one beginning.

Grey Power

To sip a cup of Earl Grey tea.
To dip into Gray's *Elegy*.
To dance at midnight
with the Grey Ladies
– as they call those nine stones
of Harthill Moor.

To inhale the pure
bewiderment of fog
that makes a mystery
of the mundane
with its grey halo.

To not have to say hello
to grey faces in a train
but simply bury my heart
in my paper' s grey matter.

To pop in at the Grey Squirrel
for a pint and a natter.
Then after I've had my fill,
to put behind the day's hassle
and return to my dethatched
grey stone that is my castle.

What more, I ask you,
can a man of colour ask for?

Shakespeare Addresses Tabloids
After Dark Lady Rumour

She was my dark secret, O that dark lady
whose hairs of wires sparked more than a sonnet.
Let the paparazzi probe her mystery.
How decipher night's hidden alphabet?

Let's say she was a lass unparallel'd
but I'm no kind of cur to kiss and tell.
And journalists know nought who know not this:
to be unnamed is a nameless bliss.

I'll not let on, no I'll not let on.
Let's say she was my Nile on Avon,
my badge of ebony in an ivory world,
my breathing gateway to the womb's word.

Fie on you who would have me expose her!
Let her be anon, and again anon.

Feeling the Whirlwind

(for Abdul Malik)

The griot-eye man
with the picong tongue
and head full of back-a-yardpolitics

a tall piece of Caribbean
rounding a corner of Brixton
feeling the whirlwind of London by foot

though he have a bus pass
to prove he done touch sixty
but a number eleven don't stop at Chaguaramas

And not even a kaiso poet
can ask a red double-decker
to put him off somewhere near Grenada.

Still, touching an exiled mango
in a busy metropolis
does bring home an archipelago

and a sweet tenor pan
spiralling over high-rise flats
weaves a greener horizon to his tracks.

Straight-talking Weatherman

It's goodbye the twenties
It's hello the teens
The temperature's dropping
Summer has become a has-been.

That grey cloud's coming
and it's got England's name on it
Nothing to write home about
unless you hate cricket

Expect showers of blessing
that don't discriminate.
If you don't like my forecast
you can always emigrate.

That dense patch means business
and thunderclouds are polyglots
Observe how they're heading north
to talk to the Welsh and the Scots.

So good news for ducks and plants
but for Brits, white and black,
it's goodbye those unionjack shorts
it's hello brolly and mack.

And if you must go out into that wind
you're a better man than me Gunga Din.

Broad Thoughts from Home

Oh to be in England
now that January's here,
and whoever wakes in England
give thanks for thermal underwear
that braces you for the bracing freeze
that distils its chill with democratic ease
between the black, the white, the brown,
not asking why or how
in England – now!

And after January, when Feb's frost follows
and the eye feasts on budding willows!
Though the streets are lined with icy views,
the little cuckoo brings its greener news.
Oh if only dear old Browning
whose genes they say had brown in
could see England's browning offspring.

The ancestry of both Robert Browning and Elizabeth Barrett has
been linked to plantation owners in Jamaica. Robert Browning's
father, the story goes, was so dark-complexioned that he was asked
to sit in the black section of the congregation in a church in St Kitts.

Dr Johnson, a Jamaican and a Dictionary (1755)

A harmless drudge, a lexicographer.
What shall I do without Francis Barber,
my Jamaican-born companion,
less a servant than an adopted son?
Yet the signs in those transatlantic eyes
tell me that he won't be patronised.
How vile to me is that word slavery
which I must define for my dictionary,
binding conscience to concise definition.
And what would this dull labour of language
mean to ones still born in voiceless bondage?
Ah well, Francis, pour me another one.
Let us drink to the next insurrection
when words unsettle iron's tyranny.

Toussaint L'Ouverture Acknowledges
Wordsworth's Sonnet 'To Toussaint L'Ouverture'

I have never walked on Westminster Bridge
or had a close-up view of daffodils.
My childhood's roots are the Haitian hills
where runaway slaves made a freedom pledge
and scarlet poincianas flaunt their scent.
I have never walked on Westminster Bridge
or speak, like you, with Cumbrian accent.
My tongue bridges Europe to Dahomey.
Yet how sweet is the smell of liberty
when human beings share a common garment.
So, thanks brother, for your sonnet's tribute.
May it resound when the Thames' text stays mute.
And what better ground than a city's bridge
for my unchained ghost to trumpet love's decree.

...Thou has left behind
Powers that will work for thee; air, earth, and skies;
There's not a breathing of the common wind
That will forget thee; thou has reat allies;
They friends are exultations, agonies,
And love, and man's unconquerable mind.

– from Wordsworth's sonnet to Toussaint L'Ouverture,
a former slave, who led a revolution that would lay the
foundation for Haiti to become the first Black republic (1804).

Chilling Out Beside the Thames

Summer come, mi chill-out beside the Thames.
Spend a little time with weeping willow.
Check if dem Trafalgar pigeon still salute
old one-eyed one-armed Lord Horatio.

Mi treat mi gaze to Gothic cathedral
Yet mi cyant forget how spider spiral
Is ladder aspiring to eternal truth...
Trickster Nansi spinning from Shakespeare sky.

Sudden so, mi decide to play tourist.
Tower of London high-up on mi list.
Who show up but Anne Boleyn with no head on
And headless Ralegh gazing towards Devon.

Jesus lawd, history shadow so bloody.
A-time fo summer break with strawberry.

Mansfield Park Revisited

(for Edward Said)

Here no talking drum
erupts in secret fire.
Here against the stable wall
the apricot doing nicely,
and though the English sun
is another pale rider
on a mount of mostly grey,
no unpleasant business
disturbs afternoon tea,
no atlantic unrest brews
in them well-laid teacups,
no uprising ruffles
the hair under parasols.
The air is civil with cakes
and marriage proposals,
for overseas possessions
are best kept overseas
and slave revolts not
right for polite conversation
or what's considered good taste.
Here even history knows its place.

And yet them bleeding canefields
refuse to stay remote.
Antigua's bitter sugar
melts in Northampton's throat.
Beside the pretty shrubbery
old ruptures regather new roots –
a colony comes home to roost.

Cric-crac
hear dat whip crack –
no turning back.

A School Trip to Sambo's Grave, Sunderland Point

The time is past for rolling in his grave.
But he will not sleep a cherub's cold sleep.
Beyond the call of duty, a dead slave
from beyond watches what the living reap.
Is that Africa whispering in the wind
when Lancashire's showers bring their blessing,
and children who leave flowers at his cross
learn how the treasure of a name is lost?
Their innocence receives a wake-up call
to vile truths that will not stay buried long,
or muted by a vandal's loutish scrawl.
Now, where stony headland meets brooding skies,
the sea roars, birds salute the air with song,
and young minds raise their unanswerable whys.

Lie Down Mother Seacole

Lie down Mother Seacole, lie down we cried,
as bullets flew under the Crimea's sky

But your scarlet ribbon braved the battlefield
Your blue bonnet rallied to our need.

We were your white sons whose wounds you calmed
We took comfort from those West Indian hands.

To us who lay bleeding, Mother Seacole,
You were the bearer of homeblessed cures

You were a sun-filled lamp in our darkness –
A shade of hope when blood opened its door

And the colour of death was anybody's guess.

If I had nothing else to be proud of, I think my rice puddings, made
without milk, upon the highroad to Sebastopol, would have gained me
a reputation. What a shout there used to be when I came out of my little
caboose, hot and flurried, and called out, 'Rice-pudding day, my sons!'
– Wonderful Adventures of Mrs Seacole in Many Lands (1857)

Ranjitsinhji at the Crease

Darling of summer 1896.
Dusky prince of the cricket pitch.
An exotic in Cambridge blue.
This wristy moustached Hindu
with Shiva in his stance
embraced empire's stealthy dance.
Kumar Shri Ranjitsinhji to you,
aka Jam Saheb of Nawanagar.
Rajput stock in an England cap.
Wisden's willow-wizard from Jam Nagar,
how well he learnt to play across the line.
Witness to his kingdom's decline,
his politics would not impress Gandhi.
But O his leg-glance was legendary.

The first Indian to play county and test cricket for England,
he became the first batsman to score 3000 runs in a season.
Of him it has been said that he batted for Empire.

By Liverpool Docks I Sat Down

To a chorus of birds winging their crosses
over this breezy archives of water
shadowed by hidden profits and losses.

What invisible shroud are they weaving?
I shouldn't be asking such questions.
Who am I to presume they're grieving?

Why don't I just enjoy the dockside view,
the fresh autumn air that expects no answer
to what history itself cannot undo?

I'll think no thoughts of triangular trade.
I'll let the swinging sixties ferry my mind
cross the Mersey to a happier decade –

when love they said was free and long hair hip
and flowers too came along for the trip.

Seaside Etiquette

The whites
sun themselves
on the pebbles.

The blacks
ensconce themselves
in the shade.

Some put this down
to genetics
I like to think
it's seaside etiquette –

a way of ensuring
an equal share
of summer's bliss
for every epidermis.

O to bask in the sun
O to bask in the shade.
Beaches mean decisions.
There's that rug to be laid.

Fairchild's Crossing

(Thomas Fairchild, 18th century nurseryman who transferred
the pollen of a sweet william into the pistil of a carnation,
creating a new plant that became known as 'Fairchild's mule'.)

Mingle dianthus barbatus
with dianthus caryophyllus
in a sort of mating dance

or if you prefer common parlance –
couple a sweet william
with a no less sweet carnation

the pollen of one
the pistil of the other
and voilà – a new creation

blooming with the blood of both

But the purists of the nation
will point a finger
from behind their greenhouses

and through a glass of distrust
they'll ask, *Has Fairchild's mule*
entered our garden?

But time will salute my genius,
my matchmaking coup,
when Europe's borders

embrace this summer darling
and the humblest of patios
flaunt my hybrid triumphs.

'Love Calls Us Back from Simplification'

(For Eavan Boland, who made this comment during a poetry reading at the Voice Box, Royal Festival Hall, April 1992.)

Out of the mouth of an Irish woman
pebbles of love play ducks and drakes
across the April face of the river Thames.

Tonight the voice will not be boxed-in
by man-made dimensions or canons of sin,
The tongue revelling in connection.

Let griot seaniche tinker obeahwoman
raise a glass to the health of contradiction.
Now Carrickfergus merge with Caribbean.

Love calls us back from simplification.

To reduce a nation to a label
To reduce a race to an assumption
To reduce a face to a formula of black and white.

To hang a stereotype around the heart
To build a wall with stones of conviction
To let the map dictate affection.

To allow boundaries their frozen dance
To grant frontiers their fixity of expression
To make a monument of an ism.

But love calls us back from simplification.
Tonight in a room above a river above a city
a poet is sharing the bread of her words

and we walking out blessed with resonance.

Coconuts' Reply

We whose insides
you brand as white
though our outsides
are wholemeal brown.

Not black enough
in talk and stride.
Too Englishified
in style and tongue.

We Coconuts
who you say talk posh.
Yuppie devotees
of a god called Dosh.

We wear no crown
of bold blackness
or flaunt with ease
our roots on our sleeves.

Like the coconut
that versatile fruit
you named us after.
We too spill water.

Crack our brown shells.
Probe our white pith.
See for yourself
how horizons sit.

Africa's fountain
waiting to be spilt
from Europe's veins.
We Coconuts.

Task of Spirit

(in memory of Stephen Lawrence, 1974-93)

Mind aglow
with the buildings you would design

architecture
dreaming in your teenage eyes

now walk among
the arcades of the heavens

where those twinkling architects
welcome you Stephen

apprentice of the sky's proportions
and now you begin

the designing task of spirit –
demolishing fixed interiors.

Wish You Were Here

A black swan fringed with white
swims on a tranquil pond.
A perfect postcard
to send to the Far Right.

Testing Time
(in memory of Ted Hughes)

October's end
has gathered more than fallen leaves
for earth's keeping

The seasons
open their door to the voice
that spoke for them

November moon
comes to harvest one who rejoiced
in its shadow

Rivers reclaim
one they consider laureate
of their blood's flow

Grasses play God
and welcome you who listened
to their requiem

Sky's granary
regains the wheat of your word-hoard's
unwritten poems

The howling wolf
gives back your name to the wind
that lent you breath

Prometheus grins
because you have returned the loan
of that fire

The fox weeps
when cunning acknowledges grief
as superior

The salmon leaps
under veils of water for this
is how they mourn

In roe-deer's eye
there is condolence and prayer
expressed as one

Thrushes lend
their choir to the hymnal air
for you their scribe

The sheep prepare
bundles of comfort for they've heard
of your coming

Over Crow Hill
nightfall embraces your black songs
as is fitting

And it is right
that oak and elm kneel in vigil
at your passing

For they stand firm
in the soil of your syllables
testing time.

Three in the Snow
(for Gillian Clarke and James Berry)

1

Cars are iced cakes
on four wheels going nowhere

trees put on their mantillas
of icicles

roofs become sloping rinks
with no hope of daredevil skate

roads turn candyfloss lakes
for dazzling jaws of headlights

phoneboxes are frosty cubicles
where your last coin

is held tenderly
as your first fire.

2

In a deluge of snowfall
whiteness pirouettes
on numbing tiptoe
and a rainbow
is an extinct creature
in this February freeze.
Even the smallest country road
aspires to the Alps.

This is weather
for sensible wellies
not ankle-low shoes.
Thank God for Gillian's boots
(which I borrow)
Survivors of Welsh valleys
granting sanctuary
to a pair of West Indian feet.

Or shall I say a pair of ravens
in a homely ark
making their covenant
with the snow-white dark?

3

This is not the humming-bird hour
when nectar secrets are revealed
and gods come disguised in tiny feathers.

No palm tree outside a window
to display a familiar majesty
as far as hungry eye can see.

Here instead a birch, a yew, an elm,
an oak maybe (I couldn't say which).
And a blackbird sits on Sylvia Plath's tree.

This is not the place where the hibiscus
dares you look inside its brazen bloom.
This is Hebden Bridge where snowbound slopes defy taxi.

And so we walk to the main road, Gillian, James and me
(thank you, brother, for the marmalade on toast and tea)
– three figures warmly wrapped in talk.

Together we walk, Jamaica, Wales, Guyana, we motley three
planting in snow our footsteps' anonymous flags.

In the Air

The buds return to twinkle the stems and winter passes.
Time for the daffodils to raise their yellow wine-glasses.

Caribbean Eye Over Yorkshire

(for John Lyons)

Eye
perched over
adopted Yorkshire.

Eye christened
in Caribbean blue
and Trinidad sunfire.

Eye tuned in
to the flame
tree's decibels

and the red
stereophonic bloom of immortelles.

Eye once a stranger
to silver birch and conifer
now on first-name terms

with beech and elm and alder.
Eye making an ally
of heather and lavender.

Eye of painter
eye of poet
eye of prankster

eye looking into linden
for ghost-traces
of silk-cotton

eye of crow
in carnival cape
seeing inward

eye of blackbird
casting
humming-bird shadow.

Trimming His Hedge

He could be just some bloke gardening
somewhere in a middle-England suburb –
one of a tribe of green-fingered locals.
But seen through anglo-saxon bifocals,
he's the immigrant trimming his hedge,
keeping his part of an unspoken pledge
to maintain a tidy distance
between citizen and citizen.

Here is home, here he took his toddling steps,
his small days no stranger to this patio,
though his turban rivals those of the tulips
that yearly register their presence
in spring's ever hopeful calendar.
And how little his spreading lavender
cares for quotas of the Home Office
or speeches built on empire's embers.

Armed with his shears under the red white and blue
he sees the flowers hoist their separate flags,
his garden diversity's great guru –
Asiatic jasmine, Algerian ivy,
African violets and English cowslips
holding out their bunch of yellow keys –
pilgrims rooted in the soil of citizenship.

On a Yazoo Stem

(for Michael Horovitz)

Bespectacled hopper
for all rhymes and seasons.
Squirrel hopper
gathering nutty poems
from Albion's unsung corners.

Runaway sunflower
climbing Blake's staircase
on a yazoo stem
grown-up still at play
with creepy-crawly friends.

I have seen you in rush-hour haste
rucksackladen yet open to embrace
bearing that vulnerable aura
that mocks a mugger's fists.

Torch-bearer schemer
of poetry olympics
not beyond elfish tricks
when the canon aims its metronome.

But beyond the halo of eccentrics
and the zany loom you weave
the hasidic child is at home
under your colourful shirt

remembering holocausts
at nations' doorsteps
yet taking hope
in a hosanna of bay leaves.

Mr and Mrs Xenophobia

Mr and Mrs Xenophobia
moved
to suburbia
aspired
to euphoria
retired
on a nest egg
of nostalgia
for Rule Britannia.

Mr and Mrs Xenophobia
closer
to their teacups and saucers
than to foreigners
closer
to their china
than to China.

Mr and Mrs Xenophobia
sufferers
from amnesia.
Now strangers
to their coronation
memorabilia.
O dearie me.
Oblivion
isn't easy
to manoeuvre.

Their condition
thankfully
is being monitored
by a dusky GP
named Abdullah.
Will their memory
ever be hunky-dory
in a land of hope and glory?

Ask Dr Abdullah.

Jet-lagged Prophets

When Jesus landed at Gatwick
his style was far from three-piece slick.
So they sniffer-dogged his hippy hair
and sandalled feet in need of washing.

When Buddha showed up at Heathrow
he was taken in for questioning.
He said he had nothing to declare
but his passport had a suspicious glow.

When Mohammed made it to Dover
they thought to themselves: asylum seeker,
though his papers were in order
and Dover not his idea of Mecca.

O jet-lagged prophets who come in peace,
what made you think it legal to be meek?
Your restless feet will know no resting ground,
when even prayers are frisked for a weapon.

By the Light of Fruits

Beside

the strawberries'
red gleam

the plums'
purple glow

the granny smiths'
green sheen

I spied
with my little eye

the bananas
in transition –

their half-yellow
glimmer

their half-ripe fingers
clenched in slowly

ripening
revelation –

a sunny salutation
from one horizon

to another.

Encounter

What makes you you
and me me?

What makes us us
and them them?

Is it the anthem
that rouses to attention?

Is it the flag
we wave on occasion?

Is it the passport
that punctuates a border?

Is it the unofficial
stamp of undeclared genes?

Is it the voice's colour
that's a dead giveaway?

Or is it the baggage
of skin and creed

that makes one say
not one of us, one of them?

And so missing the chance
of getting closer

to that image
reflected in the mirror –

yourself unmasked
in the Other's plumage.

Fallen Gold

On an ordinary
British November
autumn freely
scatters
an eldorado of leaves
for all to step on
fallen gold

and autumn
doesn't question
the origin
of those footsteps
and autumn
doesn't ask
are those boots foreign?
Do they belong
to this morning?

Autumn simply
spreads
a rug of golden brown
wind-exiled leaves
for the here-born
and the there-born

tripping both
with equal ease.